MUSEUM OF LONDON

Saxon and Norman London

John Clark

LONDON: HER MAJESTY'S STATIONERY OFFICE

CREDITS

Copyright in the illustrations lies with the Museum of London except for the following:

St Alban's church (p.14) and 'Financial Times' house (p.19), *Prof W F Grimes*; Gokstad ship (p.16), *University Museum of National Antiquities, Oslo*; Saxon building (p.20), *John Pearson*; Bayeux Tapestry (p.26), *Tapisserie de Bayeux, Ville de Bayeux*; William I's Charter (p.29), *Corporation of London Records Office*; Westminster (p.30), *T Ball/ Citisights of London*; bell (p.42), *Corpus Christi College, Cambridge*; view of London (p.44), *British Library*.

We are also grateful to the following for their co-operation:

British Museum for sword pommel (p.18); *Corporation of London Records Office* for King John's Charter (p.43), Common Seal (p.44) and Liber Custumarum (p.46); *the churches of St Bartholomew the Great* (cover) *and All Hallows-by-the-Tower* (p.10).

I would also like to acknowledge the help of many friends and colleagues and pay tribute to all who continue to throw new light on this obscure period of London's history.

John Clark
Department of Medieval Antiquities
Museum of London

British Library Cataloguing in Publication Data
A CIP catalogue record for this book is available from the British Library

Printed in the United Kingdom for Her Majesty's Stationery Office
Dd 240069 6/89   C150   3735

LONDON AD 410-1215

This book, one of a series on the history of London being produced by the Museum of London, tells a story that begins amid the ruins of the once great Roman city of *Londinium*, with perhaps a handful of impoverished inhabitants, and culminates at the beginning of the 13th century in the legend of London as 'New Troy': destined capital of England, a centre of international as well as local trade, whose people were justly proud of their city, its wealth and its independence; a city to be numbered 'among the noble cities of the world'. Unlike the stone foundations and mosaic pavements of Roman London the more ephemeral traces of Saxon and Norman timber structures did not attract the attention of 19th-century antiquarians, nor that of early 20th-century builders whose work may have entailed the destruction of such remains without record. Only recently has archaeological investigation begun to provide clues to the decipherment of some of the more obscure chapters in the story, and justified an expanded and revised new edition of a booklet first published by the museum in 1980. The implications of the new evidence, in particular for the site and nature of mid-Saxon *Lundenwic*, are incorporated and illustrated here in a history of the period in which the foundations of London's greatness as the administrative and commercial capital of England were firmly laid.

CONTENTS

Brooch of gilded silver, 6th
century. *This fine piece of jewellery
fastened the cloak of a woman who was
buried in the Saxon cemetery at
Mitcham*

THE COMING OF THE ENGLISH

The End of Roman London

In AD 410 the *civitates*, the city-based authorities responsible for local government within Roman Britain, were advised by the Emperor Honorius to take their own measures for protection against barbarian raids; no fresh troops could be sent to their aid from Rome, the hard-pressed imperial capital. Perhaps in recognition of a *fait accompli*, but with no intention that the situation should be permanent, Rome accepted the independence of Britain. So perforce did the inhabitants, most of them native Britons, Romanized Celts, though with a sprinkling of administrators and settlers from elsewhere in the empire. What measures the British took for the protection of such cities as London are not clear. London's defensive walls were no doubt in good condition, having been strengthened with towers on the east and a new wall on the river front within the previous 60 years. Yet the area within them was not densely populated. Layers of dark earth overlying earlier Roman buildings on many sites excavated in the city suggest that parts of the walled enclosure had long been used as farmland or lain waste.

The threat to Britain was from the Picts from north of Hadrian's Wall, the Irish from the west and the Saxons and related German tribes raiding across the North Sea. To face them the Roman authorities had employed mercenaries in addition to their regular troops; many of the mercenaries were from Germany, some no doubt were Saxons. Such mercenary troops, *foederati*, were granted land, which they settled with their families, in return for their

'Dark earth' at Milk Street. *Preparations for lifting a 2nd-century Roman mosaic floor; behind is a thick layer of dark agricultural soil overlying the remains of the Roman buildings*

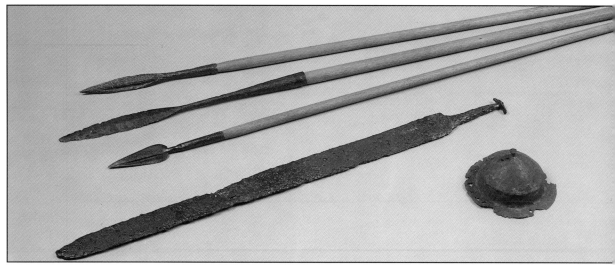

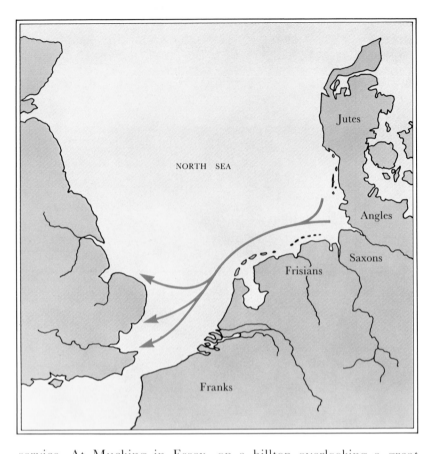

NORTH SEA

Jutes

Angles

Saxons

Frisians

Franks

service. At Mucking in Essex, on a hilltop overlooking a great bend in the Thames, where any ship-borne force moving upriver could be seen in good time, excavations have revealed a village of Saxon settlers which existed in the early 5th century, perhaps guarding the river route towards London. On the far side of the city, at Mitcham, Surrey, burials have been found indicating the presence of another Saxon settlement, and though most of the burials are later, early objects found in some of the graves suggest that a village already existed here by soon after AD 400; the same may be true of other sites, around Croydon. These could be deliberate plantations of federate troops guarding the south and south-west approaches to the Roman city.

(Left) Anglo-Saxon weapons. *Spears, a sword and an iron shield-boss*

The newly independent British authorities seem to have continued the Roman policy of employing foreign troops, with disastrous results. In the middle of the 5th century the mercenaries mutinied. In Kent, under the leadership of Hengist, they defeated a force of their former British masters at *Crecganford* (perhaps Crayford) in 457. The English chronicler who, much later, recorded the tradition of this event wrote that the British fled to London. London could certainly have served as a centre of resistance, but there is no evidence that it did. Archaeology suggests that the Roman way of life continued in London into the 5th century, and the lack of Saxon burials of this period in an area north of the city or anywhere close to it has been thought to indicate the presence of an authority strong enough to keep Saxon mercenaries and raiders at a distance, on the perimeter of a British enclave. Yet with the withdrawal of central control from Rome, the apparent collapse of provincial government and the failure of overseas trade, the dual functions of London as the administrative centre of one of the provinces into which late Roman Britain had been divided and as an international port ceased. By 457 there may have been few inhabitants, and little else worth defending. There is no account of a siege or battle; London quietly disappears from the historical record.

Anglo-Saxon Settlers

After the mercenaries came further raiders and invaders, moving inland by different routes, sometimes against stiff opposition, sometimes perhaps facing little co-ordinated resistance. The earliest English historian, Bede, writing in about 730, said that the new-comers, ancestors of the English, were Angles and Saxons from north-west Germany and Jutes from Jutland, the Angles settling in the north, the Midlands and East Anglia, the Saxons in the areas later called Wessex, Sussex and Essex, and the Jutes chiefly in Kent. Modern archaeologists, studying their culture – their pottery, their jewellery, their burial customs – and that of their continental contemporaries, reveal a more complex picture. The settlers, 'Anglo-Saxons', to use the modern term, were small, loosely-combined groups of distinct but related peoples from Germany and the North Sea coasts.

Their advance was slow, and the British long remembered the great battle at 'Badon Hill', somewhere in the West Country. Here,

Pottery cup, *c* AD 400, from the Mitcham cemetery

Saxons in the London area. *The locations of pagan cemeteries suggest that the early settlers avoided the vicinity of the Roman city of* Londinium

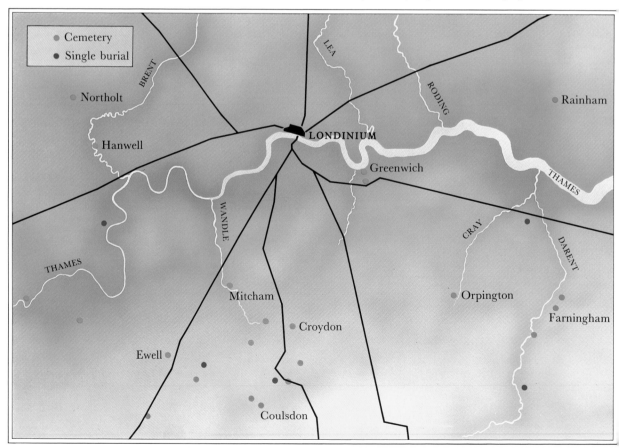

soon after 500, led according to one tradition by a general called Arthur (the King Arthur of legend), they inflicted a resounding defeat on the Anglo-Saxons, stopping and indeed reversing their progress for some 50 years. Yet by the late 6th century eastern Britain was in Anglo-Saxon hands; their war-bands were coalescing into small, independent, often warring but stable kingdoms.

Not all the British could have fled to the west or (as some did) overseas to Brittany; not all died of plague or in war. Some must have remained alongside the new settlers, or been enslaved. Anglo-Saxon men may have taken British wives. Yet they learnt little from their predecessors. The Anglo-Saxons had no use for the Roman towns with their great buildings of stone and brick. Their handmade pots replaced the factory products of the Roman world. In eastern Britain both the native British language and Latin, the official language of the empire, vanished, as did literacy. The newcomers were pagans, who brought with them their own beliefs and their own gods, of whose memory little survives now apart from the names preserved in our days of the week – Tiw, Woden, Thunor and Frig, and the names of some sacred places, such as Thundersley ('Thunor's grove') in Essex and Harrow ('shrine' or 'holy place') in Middlesex.

Few of the homesteads and villages of these early settlers have been excavated. At Mucking, for example, and West Stow (Suffolk) there were groups of small huts and some larger timber-built halls. During archaeological work in west London traces have been recorded of single small huts of the early Saxon period, apparently isolated farmsteads, but no major settlements have been identified. More often it is burial grounds which have been recognized. Since the dead were buried with things they were thought to need in the afterlife, their graves can tell much about their lives. With a man, expected to fight to defend his land and his lord, were placed his weapons: a spear, a wooden shield with an iron boss, sometimes a sword; with a woman, her household utensils and jewellery; with both, the brooches that fastened their clothing, and occasional valuable items such as glass vessels, sometimes imports from the continent. As well as at Mitcham, Saxon burials are recorded from the London area near Greenwich, around Croydon, Ewell, Hanwell and elsewhere; the settlements to which these large cemeteries belong have not been located or excavated.

Glass beaker. *From one of the 5th-century burials at Mitcham*

Remains of an early Saxon hut. *With a sunken floor and two posts to support its roof, this hut was excavated during widening of the M4 motorway at West Drayton*

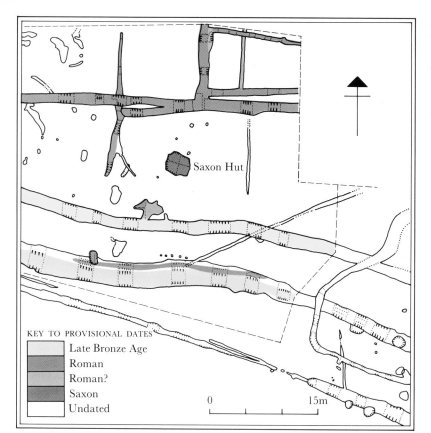

An early landscape at Harmonds-
worth, west London.
*Excavations in 1981–82 revealed traces
of a Saxon hut standing amid the
remains of Roman fields and ditches; to
the south ran a much earlier prehistoric
droveway or boundary*

Saxon Hut

KEY TO PROVISIONAL DATES
- Late Bronze Age
- Roman
- Roman?
- Saxon
- Undated

0   15m

The Fate of the City

Though the surviving Roman cities of Britain seem to have clung
to the Roman lifestyle long after 410 there is little, if any, evidence
for continuity of urban life from Roman into Anglo-Saxon times.
In London, a single 5th-century Saxon brooch was found among
the fallen roof-tiles of a Roman house excavated near Billingsgate,
a house still occupied in the early part of that century; it may
represent no more than the presence of one woman who lost her
brooch while scavenging among the ruins of the Roman city –
ruins the result not of war but of simple neglect and decay. Archaeologically London in the later 5th and 6th centuries remains a
virtual blank.

The city walls and the remains of many buildings still stood, as
they did centuries later. But the self-sufficient Saxon settlers had
no use for the centralized authority and bureaucracy which a city
represented, and perhaps were in some awe of its buildings. A
later Anglo-Saxon poet characterized the ruins of a Roman town
as 'the work of giants'. It is likely that a few people, perhaps of
British descent, perhaps Saxon, lived on among 'the work of giants'
in London, farming in the open areas; so far archaeology cannot
confirm it. As an urban centre, however, London did not exist.
Londinium, the Roman city, had died; *Lundenwic*, the Saxon port,
had yet to be born.

The end of Roman London. *The
fallen roof-tiles of a decayed Roman
building at Billingsgate; a Saxon
brooch was found among the tiles*

Two wheel-turned pots of the 6th or early 7th century. *Found in the City, they were imported from Germany or northern France*

Kent and the Franks

By the end of the 6th century most of what is now England was occupied by small Anglo-Saxon kingdoms. To the north and west were the kingdoms of the British, descendants of the Celtic citizens of the Roman province. From Strathclyde in the north to the West Welsh of Cornwall, they were little different from the kingdoms of their English enemies – though nominally at least Christian. The kings of the more settled Anglo-Saxon realms in the south-east – East Angles, Mercians, East, South and West Saxons – recognized the primacy of one king, Ethelbert of Kent. The longest-settled and richest region, favoured by its position, Kent had close links with the more advanced Germanic kingdoms of Europe. There the

Britain *c* AD. 600 *The still-expanding Anglo-Saxon kingdoms occupied the eastern part of the country; those south of Northumbria accepted Ethelbert of Kent as overlord*

Franks, conquerors of the Roman provinces of Germany and Gaul, had, unlike their kinfolk in Britain, taken over something of the culture (including the Christian religion) and the technology of those areas. Thus the industrial region around the Rhine continued to work, producing for example fine glass vessels and wheel-turned pottery, some of which found its way to Britain, perhaps in trade, perhaps as gifts between kings and nobles.

In the 580s Ethelbert of Kent contracted a political marriage with Bertha, daughter of Charibert, the Christian king of the Franks of Paris. With her his new wife brought her chaplain, and in time Ethelbert was persuaded to receive Christian missionaries to his kingdom – no doubt realizing the practical advantages of bringing England into line with the rest of Europe as much as the spiritual benefits of the new religion. Sent from Rome by Pope Gregory, a mission led by Augustine landed in Thanet in 597 and preached before Ethelbert and his assembled court. In time Ethelbert and many of his people became Christians, and Augustine was allowed to establish a church at the old Roman city of Canterbury and to build or restore others; in 601 Pope Gregory appointed Augustine as archbishop to the southern English. The Pope's original intention was that as the conversion of the English proceeded, a number of bishops would be established under two archbishops based at the Roman provincial capitals of London and York; the authority of Ethelbert, the reputation of Augustine and later setbacks in the conversion determined that the southern archbishopric should remain at Canterbury rather than being transferred to London.

All Hallows by the Tower. *This arch, built partly of tiles from a demolished Roman building, probably led from the body of the original church, perhaps founded in the 7th century, into a side-chapel*

St Paul's Cathedral

London lay in the territory of the East Saxons, whose king, Saeberht, was Ethelbert's nephew and accepted him as overlord. Under Ethelbert's influence, Saeberht agreed to receive Christian missionaries, and to allow the appointment of a bishop for his people.

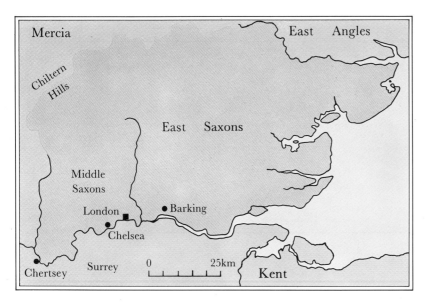

The kingdom of the East Saxons. *Showing the monasteries founded at Chertsey and Barking by Erkenwald (Bishop of London 675–693), and Chelsea, meeting place of church synods under the Mercian kings*

This was Mellitus, one of a second group of missionaries who had joined Augustine's team. However, it was Ethelbert of Kent, not Saeberht, who in 604, according to Bede, built a church in London, dedicated to St Paul, to serve as Mellitus' cathedral. Nothing is known of the first St Paul's, which presumably stood like the later cathedral on the city's prominent western hill. It may have resembled the churches built in this period in Kent, of which remains are known in Canterbury, Rochester and elsewhere; stone-built, small – about 70 or 80 feet (20–25m) long – with an apsidal (round) east end, and side chapels. However, Mellitus himself had brought advice from the Pope to the missionaries in England that where possible they should reconsecrate pagan Anglo-Saxon temples for Christian use, taking advantage of the existing veneration for such buildings, and it is possible that Mellitus' church was a converted East Saxon shrine, or stood on the site of one. A pit full of ox skulls, found during building works on the medieval cathedral in the 14th century, was thought at the time to be evidence of pagan sacrifices that had once taken place there.

Metropolis of the East Saxons

Describing the foundation of St Paul's, Bede called London the 'metropolis' of the East Saxons. However, he was writing a century and a quarter later, and archaeology provides no picture of the site or extent of this 'metropolis' in 604. Saeberht's court, like that of all Anglo-Saxon kings, would have been continually on the move. He would govern his essentially rural kingdom from any one of a number of royal houses or estates; perhaps there was one in or near London, which would encourage the establishment there of the cathedral. The few finds from the city of Frankish pottery of this period may indicate the beginnings of trade with the continent, or links between the East Saxon royal court and the Frankish kingdoms, through Kent.

The Roman city walls, more particularly perhaps the walls of the Roman fort in the north-west corner of the city, would provide a suitable defensive enclosure for a royal centre; however, the later growth of a Saxon trading town to the west, outside the walls, may suggest that it was there, as yet undiscovered, that Saeberht's palace lay. In either case, though it was increased during the periodic visits of Saeberht and his followers, the permanent population of London may have been at most a few hundred.

The conversion of the East Saxons was only superficial. On the death of Saeberht his people reverted to paganism and Bishop Mellitus fled from London. Though Ethelbert's death in 616 created a similarly dangerous situation for the Christian missionaries in Kent the Christian community survived in Canterbury, and after a year in exile the bishop returned also to the other Kentish cathedral at Rochester; but the East Saxons never accepted Mellitus back in London.

Early Saxon coins. *Silver pennies of the type known as sceattas found in excavations in the Strand–Covent Garden area*

THE EMPORIUM

The Town on the Strand

The setback to Christianity was only temporary. New missionaries came; by the mid 7th century the Northumbrians, the Mercians, the West Saxons and even the recalcitrant East Saxons had become Christian. In this period Saxon London developed into what Bede, writing in about 730, was to call an *emporium*, 'a market for many peoples coming by land and sea'. The presence of the church and the advantages of London's position, close to the borders of a number of kingdoms and at a convenient meeting point of land- and sea-routes, contributed to its growth in status, and no doubt in population, as international trade revived in more settled conditions.

As early as the 670s a royal charter referred in passing to the 'port of London where the ships land'. Until recently archaeology had failed to confirm the existence of such a port or to substantiate Bede's description of the *emporium*; then in 1988 excavations south of the Strand near Charing Cross, on the former edge of the Thames, uncovered traces of an embankment reinforced with timberwork, erected in this period. A growing number of sites north

Lundenwic. Distribution of both excavated sites and stray finds suggests that settlement in the 7th to 9th centuries was concentrated in the area of the Strand, west of the Roman city

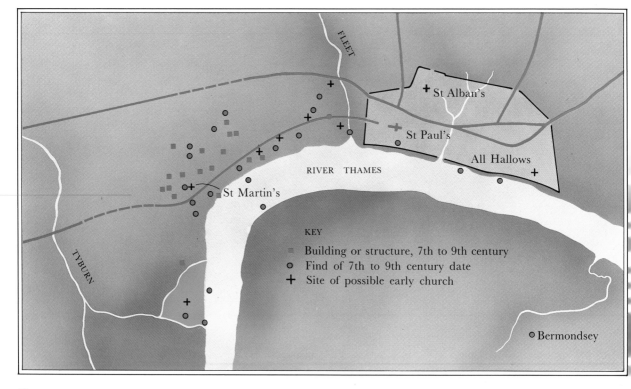

KEY

■ Building or structure, 7th to 9th century
○ Find of 7th to 9th century date
✛ Site of possible early church

FROM *LONDINIUM* TO *LUNDENWIC*

Weaving implements. *A chalk spindle-whorl and a polished bone weavers' tool, found on the site of a 9th-century building in Whitehall*

of the Strand, between Trafalgar Square and Covent Garden, have now produced traces of wooden buildings, rubbish pits and other evidence of settlement. These discoveries, together with a reassessment of earlier finds from this area, indicate the existence here in the 7th, 8th and early 9th centuries of a flourishing settlement, presumably the *emporium* of which Bede had heard. In contrast the area further east within the Roman city walls seems to have remained largely empty – apart, that is, from the cathedral; there is no evidence that the site of St Paul's was ever elsewhere. Trackways grew up through the ruins of the Roman town, linking its eastern gates and the East Saxon kingdom beyond them with the cathedral and the new town to the west. The Roman bridge across the Thames must by then have been in ruins, and no obstacle to ships moving upstream to the beaches below the settlement on the Strand.

Trade and Coinage

In documents of the 7th to 9th centuries London is referred to as *Lundenwic*, or in Latin as *vicus Lundoniae*; the Old English ending *-wic*, found also in names like Ipswich and *Hamwic* (now Southampton), means a port or trading town. International trade in northern Europe depended on a network of such ports, established under royal control and subject to royal taxes and customs tolls. Laws of Kent issued in the 670s and 680s required men from Kent buying or selling in London to report their dealings to a royal agent there; later charters from kings controlling the port of London granted freedom from toll to ships belonging to certain of their favoured subjects as a special privilege. There is also more concrete evidence of London's trade; finds from the excavations near the Strand have included fragments of imported millstones and of large wine jars from the Rhineland, as well as other pottery from northern France and Germany.

Excavating mid-Saxon London. *Emergency excavations at Jubilee Hall, Covent Garden, in 1985 revealed the slight traces of Saxon timber buildings, wells and rubbish pits*

Gold coins, the first coins to be minted in England since the Roman period, were in use by the 640s, imitating coinage already used in the Frankish kingdoms of Europe; among them were coins marked LONDUNIU, presumably minted in London. Such high-value coins were inconvenient for everyday commercial transactions, and most trade must have been by barter. Later in the century large numbers of more useful silver coins began to be issued, the first 'pennies'; though some may have been produced in London it is not until the 720s or 730s that silver coins clearly inscribed DE LUNDONIA appear. Finds of coins in England and on the continent are evidence of widespread trade among the Anglo-Saxon kingdoms and with northern Europe. English woollen cloth was probably already being exported.

Mercian London

Although nominally in the kingdom of the East Saxons, London in the 7th century seems usually to have been controlled by other

Clay loomweights and pot. *Four clay weights, used to stretch the threads on an upright loom, and this hand-made pot were found during building works south of the Strand, at the Savoy, in 1924–25 – the first Saxon material from this area to be recognized*

more powerful kings: at first of Kent, later of Mercia, the Anglo-Saxon kingdom of central England whose rulers replaced the Kentish kings as overlords in the south of the country. It was a Mercian king who in the 660s appointed a new bishop for London, though King Sebbi of the East Saxons was later buried in St Paul's Cathedral. In the 8th century Mercian kings were able to make grants of land in the London area and of trading privileges in the port without reference to the kings of the East Saxons, and perhaps founded the church that was to develop into the great medieval abbey of Westminster. Mercian royal councils sometimes met in London, and Mercian kings presided at church synods at Chelsea, perhaps a royal residence.

Of the Mercian kings Offa (757–796) was the greatest. He dominated most of southern England and directed the building of the mighty dyke that bears his name to mark and guard his western frontier with the British of Wales. He also seems to have had an interest in trade, issuing a new currency and corresponding with the Frankish King Charlemagne about the safety of English merchants abroad. Later tradition held that he had a palace in London, in the north-west corner of the Roman city, and that the church of St Alban's Wood Street was his royal chapel. However that may be, it was through the merchant settlement outside the Roman walls to the west that Mercian foreign trade must have passed. In 811 London was described as a 'famous place and royal town'. But there was a price to pay for its fame.

St Alban's, Wood Street. *Excavations on the site of this City church revealed the foundations of the little Saxon church, perhaps that of the Mercian King Offa*

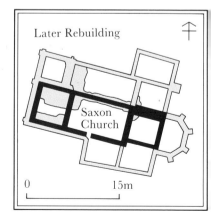

Silver penny of King Alfred.   *The reverse of this coin has a monogram made up of the letters of* LVNDONIA — *London*

The Great Army

At the end of the 8th century *vikings*, sea-raiders from Scandinavia, began attacking the coasts of northern Europe, plundering towns and monasteries. Their swift ships carried them far inland along English rivers. English chronicles record 'great slaughter' at London in 842; a hoard of silver coins buried at the Temple about then may be a relic of the attack. In 851 a force of 350 viking ships stormed London and Canterbury. *Lundenwic* could not survive many such attacks, nor the disruption of trade caused by raids elsewhere.

At first the attackers came only in summer, but by the 850s they were regularly camping each winter on English soil. In 865 a 'great army' of Danes gathered in East Anglia. In a series of annual

Viking raids

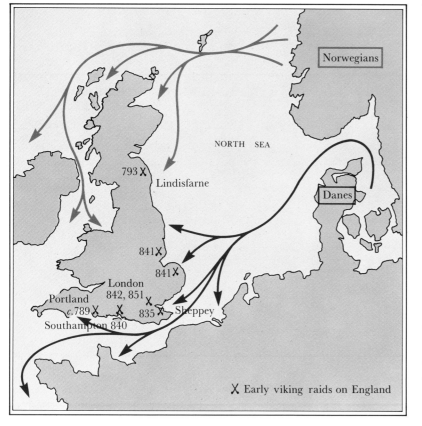

The Gokstad ship. *Preserved in the Viking Ship Museum in Oslo, this 9th-century Norwegian ship is the sort of seagoing craft used by the viking raiders*

Alfred and the Danelaw. *In 886
King Alfred and the Dane Guthrum
agreed on the boundary separating the
area of Danish rule, where placenames
of Scandinavian origin are still common,
from English territory with its fortified
burghs*

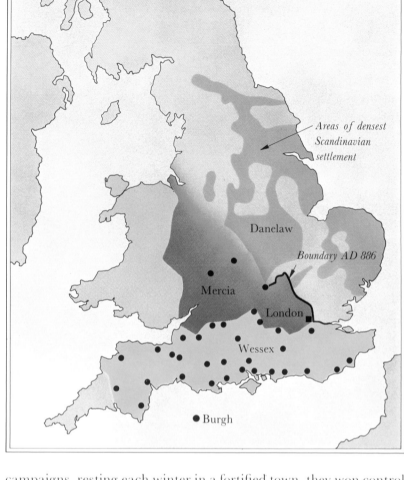

Alfred and the Danelaw. *In 886
King Alfred and the Dane Guthrum
agreed on the boundary separating the
area of Danish rule, where placenames
of Scandinavian origin are still common,
from English territory with its fortified
burghs*

Areas of densest
Scandinavian
settlement

Danelaw

Boundary AD 886

Mercia

London

Wessex

● Burgh

campaigns, resting each winter in a fortified town, they won control
of northern and eastern England, destroying the power of the
Anglo-Saxon kingdoms there. They wintered in London in 871–2.
Nothing is known of the site of their camp, nor of the fate of the
Anglo-Saxon inhabitants of *Lundenwic*. Nor is it clear whether the
army left behind an occupying force when it moved on.

The kingdom of Mercia collapsed, and its king fled. The Danes
began to settle in the lands they had already conquered and in
877 invaded Wessex, the last English kingdom to survive; the West
Saxon king, Alfred, was driven into hiding. The following year,
however, he led his troops to victory over the Danes and made a
short-lived peace with them; but further hard fighting was to follow
before Alfred finally occupied London, probably a town in ruins.
In 886 Alfred re-established London as a fortified town – a *burgh*
– and was accepted as king by all the English not under Danish
rule. In a treaty with the Danish leader Guthrum, he ceded to the
Danes the area of England later known as the *Danelaw*, north and
east of London.

Alfred's London

At about this time Alfred issued coins bearing the monogram
LVNDONIA, perhaps commemorating the recovery or the restoration

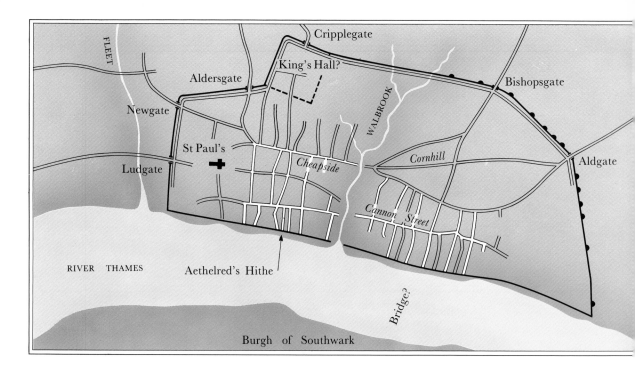

of London. But the site on the Strand was abandoned and reverted to fields, remembered only as 'Aldwych', the 'old *wic*'. Attention turned to the more easily defended area inside the Roman city walls. Alfred placed London, together with what remained of old Mercia, in the charge of the Mercian Ealdorman (lord) Ethelred, his son-in-law; a programme for the resettlement and defence of the town was begun. Overall progress seems to have been slow. As late as 898 the restoration of London was still the subject of a special meeting of the king's council held at Chelsea, the former Mercian royal meeting place.

New streets seem to have been laid out within the Roman walls. Records survive of grants made to two bishops of land at 'Ethelred's Hithe' – later the important medieval wharf of Queenhithe – complete with trading privileges; similar grants, to encourage the revival of trade as well as settlement, may have been made to other leading nobles.

Alfred and his successors established a defensive network of forts and walled towns throughout their territory. Some were on new sites, some were restored Roman cities and some were reoccupied prehistoric hill-forts. An early list of these *burghs* or boroughs includes Southwark, the 'work of the men of Surrey'; with London it could guard the Thames against Danish ships and protect the river crossing. The defence of London and Southwark would be the responsibility of the townsfolk and the inhabitants of the countryside around. The establishment of a fighting force proceeded rapidly; in 893 an army of Londoners marched out to join other English troops and capture a Danish stronghold at Benfleet in Essex, and two years later played a major part in an attack on a similar fort on the River Lea. In later years London – no longer *Lundenwic* but *Lundenburg* – was to be central to the defence of southern England.

Alfred's London. *Some documentary and archaeological evidence suggests that part of London's medieval street pattern was deliberately laid out at the end of the 9th century*

Silver-gilt sword-pommel, from Fetter Lane, Holborn

London and the King

In 911 the Ealdorman Ethelred died, and King Edward 'the Elder', Alfred's son and successor, took direct control of London 'and the lands that belonged to it', though leaving the rest of old Mercia in the hands of his sister Aethelflaed, Ethelred's widow. A campaign began to win back the territory still held by the Danes, and when in 918 Aethelflaed herself died Edward was sole ruler of a single and expanding kingdom of England. His eldest son Athelstan succeeded him, being crowned at Kingston upon Thames in 925; within two years Athelstan had conquered the last of the Scandinavian kingdoms in north-east England and received the surrender of Celtic kings in Wales and Scotland. On his coins appears the title 'King of All Britain'.

Some of Athelstan's legislation reflects the contemporary importance of London. The issue of royal coinage was strictly controlled; though it was minted in many towns the number of moneyers in

Saxon buildings. Sites in the City where Saxon or Norman wooden buildings have been revealed by excavation

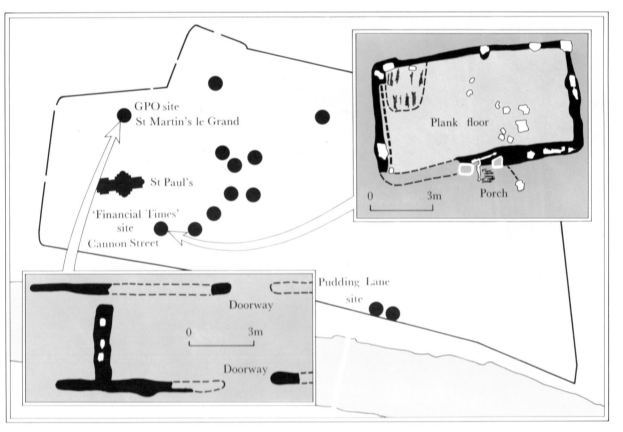

GPO site
St Martin's le Grand

St Paul's

'Financial Times' site
Cannon Street

Plank floor

0   3m   Porch

Doorway

0   3m

Doorway

Pudding Lane site

each was to be limited. London was allowed eight, more than any other, but it was followed closely by Winchester and Canterbury. It did not yet have the pre-eminence over other towns it was to achieve later, and was far from being a capital. Athelstan and his successors called their councils and issued their laws at London or any other convenient centre. Their London palace was perhaps where later legend was to place that of King Offa, defended by the walls of the old Roman fort in the north-west of the city where the street name 'Aldermanbury' may recall the residence of the Ealdorman Ethelred.

London was governed for the king by his *portreeve*, his 'town-agent' responsible chiefly for collecting the royal taxes and revenues. Royal decrees concerning London were addressed jointly to the portreeve and the bishop of London; they could be conveyed to the townspeople at their open-air assembly, the *folkmoot*, which met beside St Paul's Cathedral to discuss the affairs of the city. In Norman and later times London was divided into a number of

Saxon building at Pudding Lane. *The foundations of a large building, its timber base-plate laid on a row of imported millstones, revealed by excavations in 1981*

Reconstruction of the Pudding Lane building

Fragment of a stone cross. *Found built into a medieval wall at All Hallows by the Tower church. This side of the 11th-century cross shaft shows St Paul, with his sword, and St Peter, with his keys*

Late Saxon pottery. *Two cooking pots and a pitcher with a spout, made of shelly clay, and perhaps brought by river to London from the Oxford region*

wards, each administered by an *alderman*. The words are Anglo-Saxon, but it is not clear how early the system began.

The law-codes of the English kings were complex, but locally law-enforcement was left very much to private initiative. In the London area there was a *peace-gild*, a voluntary association of men of London, Middlesex and neighbouring areas for mutual aid, the pursuit of thieves and the compensation of their victims. This area may be 'the lands that belonged to' London in the days of King Edward, whose inhabitants had to supply labour for the upkeep of its walls and troops to defend it.

London's Buildings

There is growing archaeological evidence for the appearance of the town. There are signs that parts of the Roman city ditch were recut for defence, but the Roman walls and gates seem to have continued in use. Street surfaces of gravel have been recorded underlying the later streets in one or two places. Recent excavations have revealed remains of dozens of buildings of the 10th and 11th centuries: sunken-floored huts and outhouses; buildings with an upper floor over a cellar; more substantial structures with a wooden frame erected at ground level. None found so far were particularly grand; all were of timber. The stone and brick that might have been salvaged from the ruins of Roman buildings were apparently ignored for domestic buildings, though a building at Pudding Lane was erected on foundations made partly of unused imported millstones. Shallow wells were dug, as were cesspits and rubbish pits.

Stone seems to have been reserved for churches. Nothing is

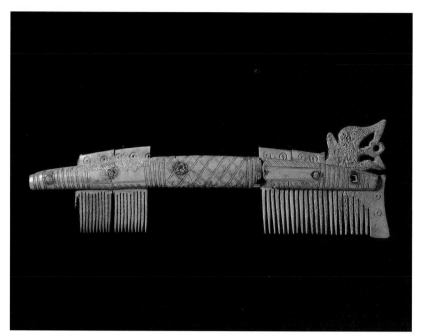

Bone comb. *Carved at one end (originally both) with a stylized animal head*

A Saxon jeweller's stock. *Part of a group of pewter brooches, beads and rings found in Cheapside, the unfinished products of a London jeweller.*

known of the greatest of these, the 'minster' of St Paul's, totally lost under the later cathedral buildings on the site. Many other smaller churches were being built, some as the private chapels of London landowners for the use of their families, servants and tenants. All Hallows Gracechurch in Lombard Street – 'Grace-church' from its thatched roof of 'grass' – seems to have been such a church; in the 1050s its owner and (probably) builder Brihtmaer gave it, together with the right to appoint the priest and collect tithes, to Canterbury Cathedral. Some churches were of wood; a document refers to 'the old wooden church of St Andrew' in Hol-born. None, either of wood or stone, survive except as foundations or fragments, as at St Bride's in Fleet Street or the traces of St Nicholas Shambles (Newgate Street) recorded in excavations. However, remains of a decorated stone cross of the early 11th century preserved in the crypt of All Hallows by the Tower show the quality of the ornamentation to be found in London's late Saxon churches.

Carpenter's axe. *Thrown away when its blade was broken, this wooden-handled axe was found in an 11th-century pit at Milk Street*

Trade and Industry

Streets seem to have been laid out around west and east market areas, 'West Cheap' (now Cheapside) and 'East Cheap'. The discovery of a stock of unfinished pewter jewellery in Cheapside may indicate that already by the 11th century Cheapside was a centre for the jewellers' and goldsmiths' crafts as it was in medieval and later times. The London goldsmiths were responsible for engraving the dies for the royal coinage, and supplying them to mints in other towns. Though little of their work in gold or silver survives, there are many examples of other decorative metalwork. Much of it shows the influence of Scandinavian art, with extravagant interlace

Knife, from Putney, 10th century. *It is inlaid with a herring-bone pattern in silver and copper, and with a silver plate with the owner's name, 'Osmund'*

patterns of beasts and foliage; similar designs appear on more everyday items of bone and leather. Other crafts are also represented archaeologically; loomweights, for example, reveal the presence of weavers making woollen cloth for home use or for export.

As well as local products the markets and wharves of London handled international trade. An English writer at the end of the 10th century, Aelfric, listed the exotic goods a merchant might carry: silks, precious stones, gold, wine, (olive) oil, ivory, bronze, glass and other luxuries. But a set of royal ordinances a little later mentions some of the more ordinary cargoes on which customs duty was payable at Billingsgate, one of London's chief wharves: timber, cloth, fish, chickens, eggs and dairy produce. Besides the local women dealing in cheese and butter (and paying two pence a year for the privilege) there were merchants from Normandy, northern France, Flanders and Germany. The foreign merchants were buying wool, which along with cloth was England's main export and source of wealth in the middle ages; agricultural produce, fine metalwork and embroidery, and silver, usually in the form of coinage, were also exported.

Even before the wars of the 11th century placed a Danish king on the throne of England, the existence in the eastern half of the country of the Danelaw, largely Scandinavian in population, law and culture though ruled by the English king, encouraged links with the Scandinavian countries. The vikings who had terrorized northern Europe opened up trade routes along its coasts, and there were Scandinavian trading posts and settlements from the great rivers of Russia to Iceland, Greenland and, briefly, North America. London was in contact with this network of trade, and excavation produces Baltic amber, carvings in walrus-tusk ivory from the Arctic and whetstones of a particularly suitable stone found only in southern Norway. In the other direction a pewter brooch has been found in Dublin which was made in the same mould as one in the group from Cheapside; the Cheapside jeweller clearly had contacts with the viking merchant town there. Most of the products of the north, such as fish, furs, timber and rope, do not survive well on archaeological sites. Nor do many of the luxuries from the south and east that Aelfric lists, though fragments of glass vessels imported from Syria have been found.

It was the Thames that provided London's access to foreign trade. Single-masted ships – the Billingsgate customs list refers to the larger vessels as *keels* and *hulks* – made the North Sea and Channel crossings and came upriver with the tide, while smaller rivercraft carried local trade. Planking from a small vessel of this period was recovered from excavations near Billingsgate. Here and elsewhere reinforced embankments of clay were laid down at which ships could be berthed. The river-crossing – the earliest definite references to a bridge seem to be in the late 10th or early 11th century – made London a convenient place to tranship goods to or from land transport, and London's wharves would have been busy with ox-carts and pack-horses. But in the early 11th century the bridge and the wharves were also the objective of seafarers very different from the merchants of Scandinavia, France or Germany.

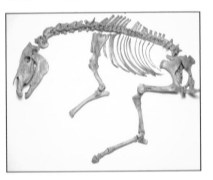

Skeleton of a horse. *Found in a 10th-century pit at Ironmonger Lane, the bones are those of a small horse, about 13½ hands*

DANISH AND ENGLISH KINGS

New Danish Attacks

Towards the end of the 10th century a new series of attacks from
Scandinavia began. The usual piratical raids quickly developed
into a purposeful campaign to win back the Danelaw and gain
political control over England. London was the focus of much of
the fighting that followed. In 994 Swein Forkbeard, son of the king
of Denmark, and the Norwegian Olaf Tryggvason led an assault
on the town, which held out with a determination that surprised
the attackers. Over the next 20 years London was attacked time
and time again; 'but praise God, still it stands safe and sound', an
English chronicler commented in 1009. Fighting centred around
the riverside and the bridge which barred the river. A later historian recorded an attack in which Olaf Haroldson, afterwards
King Olaf (the royal saint) of Norway, destroyed the bridge –
though the obscure poem that inspired this account may describe
an attack on the 'wharf' rather than the 'bridge' of London. The
Dane Cnut found the bridge so well defended in 1016 that he was
forced to drag his ships around it along a channel dug through
low-lying ground at its southern end, before he could lay siege to
the town.

However, English resistance was gradually overwhelmed. In
1014 Swein Forkbeard, now ruler of Denmark, died during a suc-

Viking battle-axes and spears from
the Thames at London Bridge.
*Perhaps the result of a battle, or
thrown into the river as an offering to
the gods*

cessful campaign in England, and the Danish invaders chose his son Cnut as their leader. By the end of 1016 the English King Ethelred and his eldest son Edmund were both dead, and Cnut, with whom the men of London had already bought a separate peace, was accepted as king of all England. During the wars the invaders had often been bought off by payments of *danegeld*; similar payments continued, converted into a regular tax to pay for a standing army and fleet. Something of London's wealth is indicated by the fact that in 1018 the city was taxed the huge sum of 10,500 pounds in silver to pay off Cnut's seamen.

Edward the Confessor

For 25 years Cnut's family ruled England. Many of his court were of course of Scandinavian origin, and there was strong northern influence on England's law, language, culture and art. But in June 1042 King Harthacnut, Cnut's son, died suddenly 'as he stood at his drink' at a wedding-feast in Lambeth. He had no son to succeed him, and by popular decision the crown was offered to Edward, surviving son of the English King Ethelred.

Edward had spent much of his life in exile in Normandy at the court of the dukes Richard (his uncle) and Robert, Richard's son. Nicknamed 'the Confessor' ('the priest'), he was a man of great piety. In his later years he devoted much of his energy and much of the royal income to the building of a new abbey dedicated to St Peter – Westminster, the 'west monastery', on an island in the marshy mouth of the River Tyburn where it entered the Thames 1½ miles (2km) west of London. There had long been a church here, perhaps from the days of King Offa of Mercia, and a small community of monks. Edward reorganized the monastery, granting

Stone slab from a monumental tomb. *Erected at St Paul's, perhaps for a member of the court of the Danish King Cnut, it is carved with an inscription in the Norse runic alphabet. The runes read* KINA LET LEKIA STIN THENSI AUK TUKI *('Ginna and Toki had this stone laid')*

London and Westminster. *The siting of Edward the Confessor's new palace*

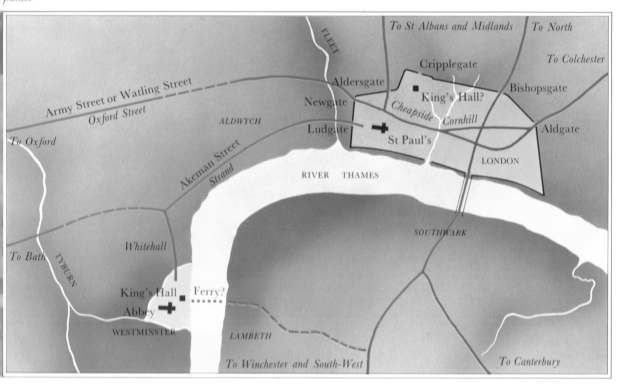

SIC PORTATVR:CORPVS:EADWARDI:REGIS:AD:ECCLESIAM:S(PETRI A

The consecration of Westminster Abbey and the funeral of King Edward. *Shown on the 11th-century Bayeux Tapestry*

it large new estates, and had a great new church built, in the style of the churches he had seen in Normandy.

Unlike his predecessors Edward chose to call his royal councils to meet at only a few major centres – usually London or Gloucester, or sometimes Winchester. Next to his new church at Westminster he built himself a royal hall. Any royal residence situated inside the walls of London seems to have been abandoned at this time; at Westminster Edward had his palace and his church, the abbey, a royal centre distinct from the busy commercial city. In the long term his decision to establish his palace there would lead to the development of London and Westminster as twin but separate centres, one of trade and industry and one of government and law.

Just after Christmas 1065 the abbey church was consecrated; a week later Edward was dead. He was buried in his new church, where his tomb became a shrine and a place of pilgrimage. He left an unsettled kingdom. He had no heir, and had apparently promised the throne both to the Norman Duke William, son of his cousin Robert, and to the English Earl Harold of Wessex, who had governed much of England on his behalf for 10 years; meanwhile the Scandinavians awaited the opportunity to launch a new invasion.

1066

The English leaders quickly elected Earl Harold as king. The catastrophic events of the year 1066 followed. In September Harold led the English to victory over an invading Norwegian force in Yorkshire, only to learn that William of Normandy had landed with his army on the south coast. Once more, as in the days of Alfred, the men of London marched out with the king's forces to meet the invader. This time, on 14 October near Hastings, they were defeated, their king killed. The English retreated to London, which they hoped to hold. William's advance was slow. He was wary of the well-defended city, particularly after his vanguard was driven back from the south end of the bridge, and led his troops in a wide loop round to the west, cutting London off. At last at Berkhamsted in Hertfordshire the English surrendered; among the English nobles who offered William the throne were 'all the best men from London'. On Christmas Day at Westminster Abbey William was crowned king.

The Tower of London. *The model in the Museum of London shows the White Tower as it may have appeared in the late 11th century soon after its building*

The Norman City

THE NORMANS

William and London

Faced with what was described as 'the restlessness of its large and fierce populace' William built castles to control London. One was probably that known later as Baynard's Castle, on the west side of the town, south of Ludgate. With an adjacent castle, the Tower of Montfichet, it dominated St Paul's Cathedral, symbolic centre of the city, and the road to Westminster. Eventually, some 200 years later, these two castles were to be demolished and their sites forgotten; however, William also started work on a better-known and longer-lived castle in the south-east corner of London, where the Roman city wall was repaired to defend the site on the east and on the riverside. The fortification was completed on the north and west, facing the rest of the town, by a new palisade and a ditch. Soon, before 1080, work began on a more substantial structure within this enclosure, a fortified palace of stone, the White Tower. Gradually over the next 200 years the walled area around it was extended, creating the great concentric fortress, the Tower of London, that still stands.

In charge of London, as portreeve, William placed one of his

William I. *The formalized portrait of the king, with crown and sceptre, on a silver penny*

St John's Chapel, Tower of London. *The White Tower was a fortified royal palace, and included within it a royal chapel, shown here in a 19th-century engraving*

leading supporters, Geoffrey de Mandeville, who may have governed the city from the Tower. But the Norman king's attitude to London was not wholly one of repression. An early document addressed to the portreeve Geoffrey – jointly with the Bishop of London as in Anglo-Saxon days – was a 'charter', a formal letter from the king, guaranteeing the citizens's rights:

> William the king greets William the bishop and Geoffrey the portreeve and all the citizens in London, French and English, in friendship. I inform you that I intend you to have all the rights in law you had in the days of King Edward, and each child to be his father's heir after his father's day; and I will not allow any man to do you any wrong. God keep you.

Riverside wall at the Tower of London. *The late Roman wall that defended the city on the Thames side was refurbished by the Normans to serve as the southern wall of their new castle.*

William I's charter to the citizens of London

Friendly in tone, though perhaps vague as to the privileges it offered, it confirmed that there would be no further confiscation of property. It demonstrates the caution with which William approached his wealthiest and most populous town and the care he was willing to take to conciliate its citizens.

In spite of the building of the new castles, London's royal centre remained at Westminster, and in 1097–99 William's son, King William II, built a new hall to replace that of Edward the Con-

Norman castles in London. *The sites of the Tower and Baynard's Castle*

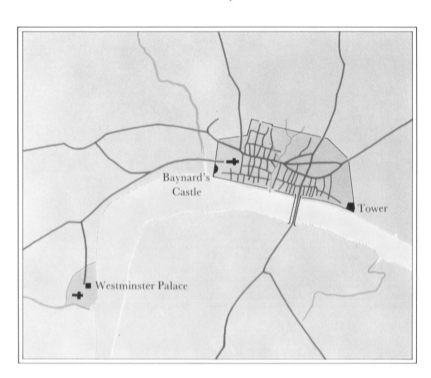

fessor. It was very large, about 240 feet (75m) long, with stone walls and a wooden roof probably supported on two rows of columns; with a new grander roof added in the 1390s Westminster Hall survives today.

Domesday Book

Like their Anglo-Saxon predecessors the Norman kings had no single capital. It was from Gloucester that in 1085 William issued orders for a survey of his kingdom, and to Winchester, the old West Saxon royal city, rival to London as meeting-place of the Norman royal court, that the returns came in during the following year. From this survey two volumes were compiled, making the so-called 'Domesday Book': a register of landholders, of rents and of the economic potential, largely agricultural, of each estate. From it can be derived a picture of the economic geography of 11th-century England: an essentially rural country with a population of around 1½ million, few towns having more than 2000 inhabitants. The Domesday statistics for the countryside were recorded systematically; the complex organization of a town seems largely to have defeated the surveyors. London and Winchester were omitted, except for incidental references. For London we hear only of the properties there that belonged to rural estates and were assessed alongside them – the 28 houses paying nearly 14 shillings in rent to Barking Abbey, for example. Such properties would provide a Norman landowner not merely with a rental income but with access to London's markets and a town residence at any time he had business at the king's court.

More complete is the view to be derived from the Domesday survey of the countryside around London. Such places as 'Stebenhede' (Stepney) and 'Chenesitun' (Kensington) were already well-established farming villages with arable land, woods and grazing for cattle and pigs, while riverside settlements like 'Fuleham' had fishing rights on the Thames. Some of the surplus produce of field and river must have found its way to London for sale, to feed a town population that by now may have reached 10,000 or even 15,000.

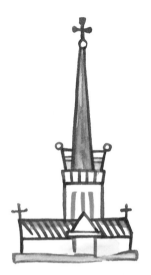

St Paul's Cathedral. *The cathedral's spire already dominated the city's skyline when Matthew Paris, a monk of St Albans, drew this sketch of it in the 1250s*

Cathedral and Parish Churches

In 1087 one of the many fires from which London suffered destroyed St Paul's Cathedral. The original church of 604 would have undergone much extension and rebuilding in the Saxon period – there had been at least one earlier fire and subsequent rebuilding, in 962; nothing is known of the shape or size of the church that perished in 1087. Rebuilding quickly began, aided by royal patronage, but was to drag on for many years. There was another fire in the 1130s, which delayed the work, but by 1148 the eastern arm, the choir, which probably had an apsidal end, was complete. Work on the western arm (the nave) and the north and south transepts continued; for over 50 years these must have had temporary wooden roofs, for their stone vaulting was not completed

St Paul's Cathedral. *An engraving, made shortly before the destruction of the medieval cathedral in the Great Fire of 1666, shows the view eastwards along the magnificent Norman nave*

until early in the 13th century, as was the central tower with its great lead-clad timber spire rising about 450 feet (140m) above the city. In 1256 work began to extend the choir eastwards and remodel it in the new Gothic style; the enlarged church, one of the finest of English cathedrals, survived until the Great Fire of 1666.

As the spire of St Paul's dominates early illustrations of London, so the cathedral dominated much of city life. The precinct around it contained church buildings, the bishop's palace and, according to later tradition, the meeting place of the folkmoot. The figure of St Paul appeared on the city's seal in the 13th century and, according to one description, on the banner which the men of London carried into battle. The bishop and the cathedral authorities owned property all over the city and large estates in Middlesex (Stepney, Willesden and Fulham, for example) and around, including the castle and town of Bishop's Stortford in Hertfordshire.

Writing in the 1170s William Fitz Stephen reckoned that besides St Paul's there were in the city and its suburbs 13 monastic churches and 126 parish churches. Medieval statistics are notoriously unreliable, and it is difficult to define the area of the 'suburbs' in such a way that these figures are accurate. Certainly by William Fitz Stephen's time there were about 100 parish churches within the city wall. They were small, most serving a compact community of neighbours, the parish boundary defined by the back walls of their properties. Parishes in the centre of the town were tiny, those in the less densely populated outskirts were larger. Some churches were clearly founded by a landlord for the use of his family and tenants. Some of them, like St Mary Woolnoth ('Wulfnoth') bear their founders' names as an addition to that of the saint. In the 12th century, a time of church reformation and reorganization, these private churches, where the owner himself appointed the priest, tended to pass into the hands of cathedral or monastic authorities.

Bronze hanging lamp. *From the site of St Martin's-le-Grand. This oil lamp may have hung over the altar of the monastic church of St Martin's*

Bermondsey Abbey. *Excavations on the site of the abbey, founded in 1089, revealed the great drain serving the latrine of the infirmary building*

Monasteries and Hospitals

A feature of the medieval church, and one that was increasing in importance in the 11th and 12th centuries, was the monastic system, where closed communities of men or of women lived a religious life according to a rule or order, free of responsibilities to a parish, but sometimes carried out other spiritual or social duties for the benefit of people at large. The 13 monastic houses that William Fitz Stephen counted must have included two founded before the Norman conquest: the Abbey of St Peter (Westminster), which under royal favour, as the chosen place of coronation of all the kings from Harold and William I on, was growing immensely in wealth and importance; and St Martin's-le-Grand, inside the city wall near Aldersgate – not large, but important as a sanctuary, an island within the city not subject to the legal control of the civic authorities. Others were set up in the late 11th and the 12th centuries on open land on the edge of the city and in the countryside around: at Bermondsey in 1089; at St Mary Overy, Southwark; at Holy Trinity, Aldgate – founded by Matilda, wife

Holy Trinity Priory, Aldgate.
Remains of a side chapel of the 12th-century priory church revealed in excavations in 1984, and later lifted for preservation.

of Henry I, in 1108, and supported by some of the most important men of London – and at St Bartholomew, Smithfield. Early in the 12th century a nunnery was founded at Holywell, Shoreditch, and another, dedicated to St Mary, at Clerkenwell.

Next to St Mary's Clerkenwell stood the Priory of St John, founded by the Knights Hospitallers; the similar and rival order of Knights Templars established their English headquarters near Holborn in 1128, later moving to a new site by the river, where their church, with a circular nave in imitation of the Church of the Holy Sepulchre in Jerusalem, still stands. These two military orders were founded to win back the Holy Land from the Saracens

Temple Church. *The ornately carved west doorway of the late 12th-century church of the Knights Templar in Fleet Street*

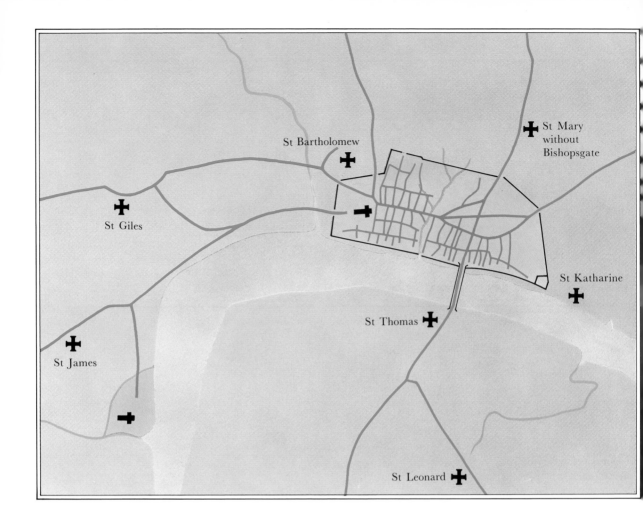

and to guard the pilgrim routes. The Templars, an extremely wealthy order, were noted as bankers and financiers; their London precinct housed a royal treasury for many years.

The church provided care for the sick and the needy. 'Hospitals', some to house the sick, some as refuges for the poor or hostels for travellers, were established under ecclesiastical control, and royalty, nobles and townsfolk made donations and bequests for their upkeep and for the good of their own souls. Little medical treatment was given; the care rather than the cure of the sick was their function. Of the hospitals that of St Bartholomew, adjacent to the priory, is the best-known and longest surviving; others included St Mary's, outside Bishopsgate, the 'New Hospital' founded by the Londoner William Brown and his wife Rose, on which work started in 1197.

Two 11th-century bishops of London had died of leprosy, a disease known and feared throughout Europe. Sufferers were outcasts, driven from towns, forced to beg for their food. Around London a ring of leper hospitals grew up as refuges for lepers expelled from the city or passing along the main roads. The first was that at St Giles' (Bloomsbury), founded and endowed by Queen Matilda. Her example of charity was followed by many others.

The Guildhall of the Men of Cologne. *Remains of a wall, excavated in 1988 beneath Cannon Street Station, on the site occupied by traders from Cologne in the 12th century, and the later Steelyard of the Hanseatic merchants.*

Foreign pottery imported into London in the 11th to 12th centuries. *A grey-ware 'ladle' and a pot with painted decoration from the Rhineland and a yellow-glazed spouted pitcher from what is now Belgium*

(*Left*) Seal of St Bartholomew's Hospital. *This impression of the early official seal of the hospital shows a figure of St Bartholomew with his hand raised in blessing*

Merchants and Immigrants

By the end of the 12th century London's population may well have grown to over 30,000 and included an increasing number of foreign immigrants and transient visitors. Merchants from Rouen had already been involved in commerce in London before the Norman conquest, but further settlers from the Norman kings' French domains followed the invaders. 'Many natives of the chief Norman cities, Rouen and Caen', as a 12th-century writer explains, 'settled in London as the foremost town in England, because it was more suited to commerce and better stored with the goods in which they were accustomed to trade'. German traders had long travelled the routes linking Thames and Rhine, and in the 12th century the 'men of Cologne' had a 'house' or 'guildhall' by the Thames, their permanent London headquarters and trading-post.

Among other businessmen attracted to London were Jews. The

first Jewish settlers seem to have come from Rouen, where a long-established Jewish colony had been attacked and many Jews killed in 1096. Forbidden by Christian law from themselves engaging in trade or industry they provided financial backing for others. They acted as money-lenders to merchants, nobles and kings, and so obtained grudging royal protection. By 1130 there was a London community led by Rabbi Joseph, centred on 'Jews' Street' (Old Jewry). Until 1177, although there were Jewish residents in many English towns, only in London were they allowed a cemetery, outside Cripplegate, to which all Jews who died in England were brought for burial. Jews were regarded as aliens, not integrated into English society. Kings were ever eager to find excuses to extort money from them, while they attracted the envy, sometimes the fear, of their Christian neighbours – who in any case might be in debt to them. In 1189 an incident at the coronation of Richard I sparked off a riot in which the London Jewry was burnt and 30 Jews were killed. Similar violence occurred elsewhere, and Jews were never safe from extortion and intimidation.

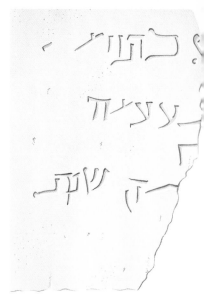

Fragment of a Jewish tombstone commemorating 'Nahum'. *Found in 1753 built into the medieval city wall where it had been used for repairs. The stone has since been lost*

The crypt of the Prior of Lewes' house, Southwark, before its demolition

Town Houses

During the events of 1189 Jews took refuge in their stone houses in the Jewry. Other wealthy merchants must have had similar houses; stone houses in Cheapside are mentioned in building regulations of 1212, and their remains have been found elsewhere in the city. They probably resembled surviving examples in Lincoln, Southampton and other towns: simple rectangular buildings with a hall – the living accommodation – on the upper floor reached by an outside staircase, a shop or warehouse below.

Most buildings, however, were of timber, like those of earlier times, with a roof of thatch. Fires could start easily and spread rapidly; in a fire in (probably) 1133 much of the city from Aldgate to St Paul's was burnt down. Though buildings were close enough

Foundations of a stone-built house in Milk Street. *Badly disturbed by modern foundations, these walls of ragstone, chalk and gravel supported the undercroft or cellar of a 12th- or 13th-century house*

The south end of Old London Bridge. *Excavations in 1984 in Southwark, just east of the modern London Bridge, revealed the south end of the bridge begun in 1176. Close-set elm piles (right) protect the upstream side of the stone bridge abutment*

together for fire to spread there were still large open areas within the city walls; but suburbs were growing up in Southwark and along the road to Westminster. According to William Fitz Stephen 'almost all the bishops, abbots and nobles of England are, as it were, citizens and townsmen of London, having their fine houses there . . .' Such men had country estates, but used their town houses when in London on business. Much larger than the houses of city merchants, these establishments would have a separate main hall, perhaps a chapel, a kitchen, accommodation for servants, stables and store-sheds. Not until the end of the 12th century did the Archbishop of Canterbury acquire his permanent London residence at Lambeth, conveniently close to the royal palace at Westminster. Much earlier the Bishop of Winchester, who owned a great deal of property in Southwark, had established a house there, on the south bank of the river opposite the city. Close to the bishop's house, a fine stone-vaulted cellar that lay beneath the hall of a large 12th-century house survived until the 19th century, when it was demolished in connection with roadworks. This house belonged in later medieval times to the Prior of Lewes, in Sussex, but it may have been built originally for the earls de Warenne, one of the most important Norman families in Surrey.

The River and the Bridge

London Bridge provided easy access from these Southwark properties to the city itself. The bridge was essential to London's existence, the only bridge across the lower Thames. The river had been bridged at just this point by the Romans; how long the Roman bridge lasted and what attempts the Saxons made to repair or replace it are not clear – it may have been superseded by a ferry for some time. Certainly by the early 11th century a bridge existed, a barrier to enemy fleets and a convenient place for collecting tolls on shipping. The bridge was of wood, prone to damage by flood, frost and fire, and in 1176 work began on a sturdier bridge of stone. A quarter of a mile long, on 19 piers with a drawbridge to allow larger ships through, it was one of the earliest stone bridges in medieval Europe, admired by all later visitors to London. The

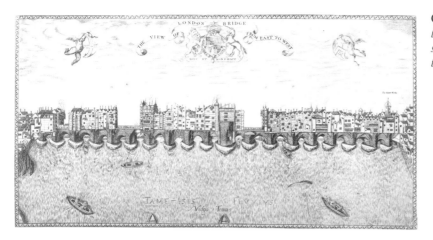

Old London Bridge. *A drawing of the bridge at the end of the 16th century shows it much as it had appeared throughout the medieval period*

building work, which continued for many years, was encouraged by King John and backed by Londoners' donations. Rents from bequests of land and the income from houses and shops built on the bridge itself paid for its upkeep. 'Old London Bridge' survived, much altered and repaired, until 1830.

Both up- and downstream of the bridge, wharves were stretching along the north bank of the river. A piecemeal development of private quays was already beginning in places in the 11th century; each landowner extended his property southwards by erecting embankments or timber revetments of increasing solidity to reclaim the foreshore and to provide moorings for new and larger ships. Smaller vessels carried considerable local trade along the Thames and on tributaries such as the Lea and the Medway. There were complaints that this traffic was being obstructed by dams built across the rivers to provide power for watermills and by fixed fish-traps, complaints that led to royal proclamations in 1197 and 1199 ordering weirs to be destroyed. Probably, like most such proclamations, they had little effect.

Late 12th- to early 13th-century waterfront. *Seen from the river side, this front-braced timber revetment was discovered in excavations close to Billingsgate, 1982–83*

Planking from an early medieval boat. *Reused in one of the waterfront revetments at Billingsgate*

THE BARONS OF LONDON

The Common Seal of London. *The seal, probably first used in about 1219, shows St Paul and is inscribed in Latin 'Seal of the Barons of London'*

City Government

Richard I's proclamation in 1197 against the obstruction of the Thames was issued 'for the common good of our city of London'. It was presumably made at the request of Londoners, users of the river. During the 12th century the influence of London's citizens and their ability to organize themselves developed considerably. They were able to buy or extort privileges from kings, embodied in a series of royal charters still preserved in the Corporation of London's Records Office. These documents are often obscure, and the steps by which during the century London achieved a considerable degree of self-government are not clear.

Royal communications were no longer addressed to the portreeve; the title *sheriff* ('shire-reeve', the king's representative in a shire or county) was adopted. We hear of *two* sheriffs, of London and Middlesex; for a while there appeared another official, the *justiciar*, apparently responsible for the administration of royal justice in the city. Londoners won the right to choose their own sheriffs for London and Middlesex rather than accepting the king's appointments; for this privilege they paid an inclusive sum of £300 each year to the royal treasury in place of piecemeal tax assessments.

The folkmoot continued to meet by St Paul's, but the complex business of administering a populous city, filled with newcomers from other parts of the king's territory, English and French, and with foreign merchants, quickly exceeded the scope of any large open meeting. Administration passed into the hands of a more select assembly of leading citizens, who acquired the title *aldermen* ('elders'), a title reserved under the Anglo-Saxon kings for their leading subjects. During the 12th century they were probably already meeting regularly in a building on the site of the later Guildhall.

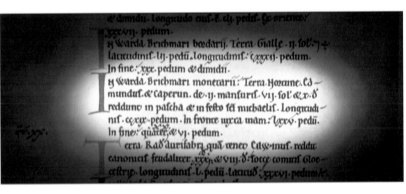

A list of lands in London belonging to St Paul's Cathedral. *This early 12th-century document lists properties according to the ward in which they lie; this entry concerns 'the ward of Brichmar the moneyer'*

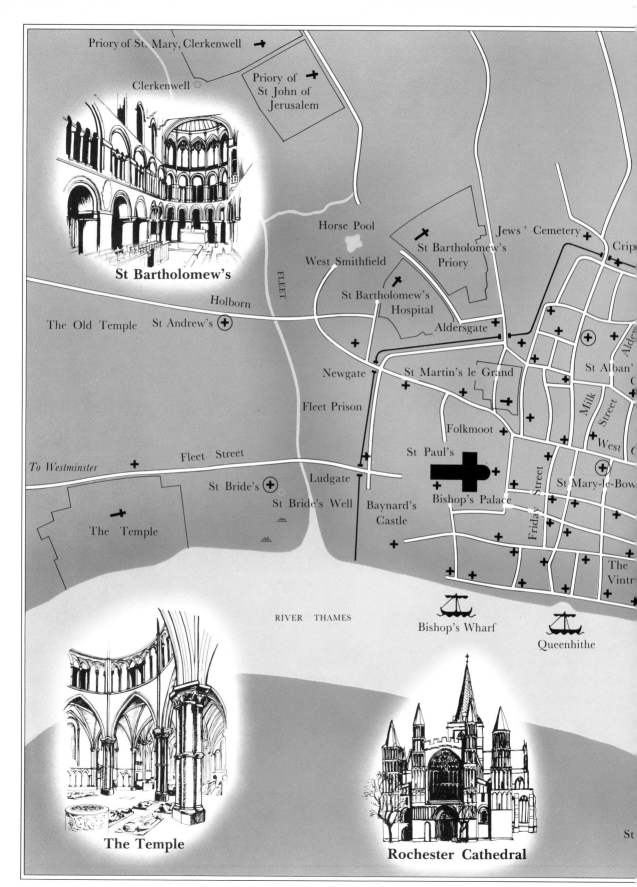

Priory of St. Mary, Clerkenwell

Clerkenwell

Priory of
St John of
Jerusalem

St Bartholomew's

Horse Pool

West Smithfield

St Bartholomew's
Priory

Jews' Cemetery

Crip

FLEET

Holborn

St Bartholomew's
Hospital

Aldersgate

St Alban'

The Old Temple   St Andrew's ✚

Newgate

St Martin's le Grand

Milk
Street

St Alban'

Fleet Prison

Folkmoot

West

To Westminster

Fleet Street

St Paul's

Friday
Street

St Mary-le-Bow

St Bride's ✚

Ludgate

Bishop's Palace

St Bride's Well

Baynard's
Castle

The
Vintr

The Temple

RIVER THAMES

Bishop's Wharf

Queenhithe

The Temple

Rochester Cathedral

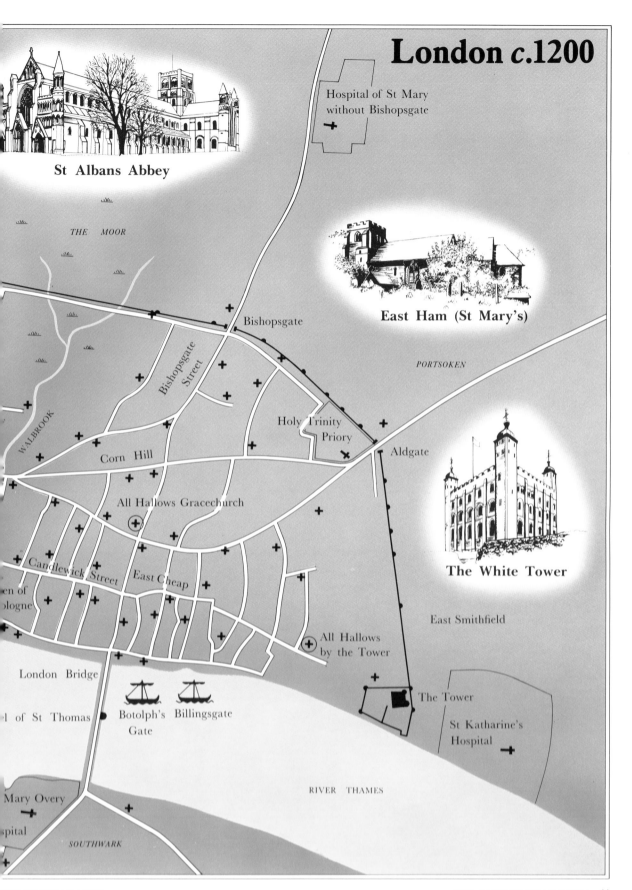

London *c.*1200

St Albans Abbey

Hospital of St Mary
without Bishopsgate

East Ham (St Mary's)

THE MOOR

Bishopsgate

PORTSOKEN

Bishopsgate Street

WALBROOK

Corn Hill

Holy Trinity
Priory

Aldgate

The White Tower

All Hallows Gracechurch

Candlewick Street

East Cheap

en of
ologne

All Hallows
by the Tower

East Smithfield

London Bridge

Botolph's
Gate

Billingsgate

The Tower

l of St Thomas

St Katharine's
Hospital

Mary Overy

RIVER   THAMES

spital

SOUTHWARK

Their assembly was the *husting*. This court – the derivation of its name from Old Norse ('house-meeting') suggests Scandinavian influence – seems to have been ruling on standard weights and measures already in the 10th century, and continued this interest in trade and the relations between merchants; its members were themselves drawn from the wealthy merchant class.

In time of war the alderman organized the city's defence; in time of peace they administered its law. By the early 12th century the city was divided into areas, *wards*, each governed by an alderman; the system perhaps had its beginning much earlier. Some of these wards may have originated in the areas of private jurisdiction over their tenants that certain large landowners held within the city. An alderman's power was personal, not conferred by election to an office. Wards were named after their aldermen, and there was a tendency for the position to remain within a family. Within his ward the alderman had considerable authority, and held his own law-court, the *wardmoot*.

The Barons and the Mayor

The aldermen were a merchant oligarchy, the leading members of a community which was referred to in documents of the period as 'the barons of London'. The term seems to embrace only those inhabitants of London who had full legal privileges and liabilities, those of status to be represented in negotiations with the king or his councillors. The commercial towns of Normandy, such as Rouen, from which some of London's merchant families came, had long had a measure of independence from royal or ducal control and were organized as self-governing communities to which the name *communes* was applied. Not surprisingly the 'barons' of London sought similar status for their own town. Kings were not eager to accept such an innovation, and it was not until 1191 that Richard I formally recognized the existence of the Londoners' 'commune'. Henceforth London was to be treated as a single community, not a group of individuals.

A French commune appointed its own chief magistrate, its *mayor*. Londoners would not be satisfied with the right merely of choosing the royal sheriffs, with such a model before them. They unofficially adopted the title 'mayor' for their chosen leader before they received royal approval. According to tradition the first mayor of London, Henry Fitz Ailwyn, took office in 1189, and he was certainly recognized as mayor by the citizens of London in the 1190s. A document surviving from 1193 is the 'Oath of the Commune': to keep faith to King Richard, to preserve the commune, and to obey the mayor. In 1202 King John referred in a charter to 'our mayor and citizens' of London, but it was not until 1215 that he finally gave formal permission for his 'barons of London' to choose themselves a mayor each year, 'faithful, discreet and fit to govern the city'.

The Gilds

Alongside the mayor, the aldermen and their court, other institutions were developing in this period that would be equally

'The bell of the commune of London'. *Drawn by Matthew Paris of St Albans in the mid 13th century, the bell which summoned meetings of the folkmoot*

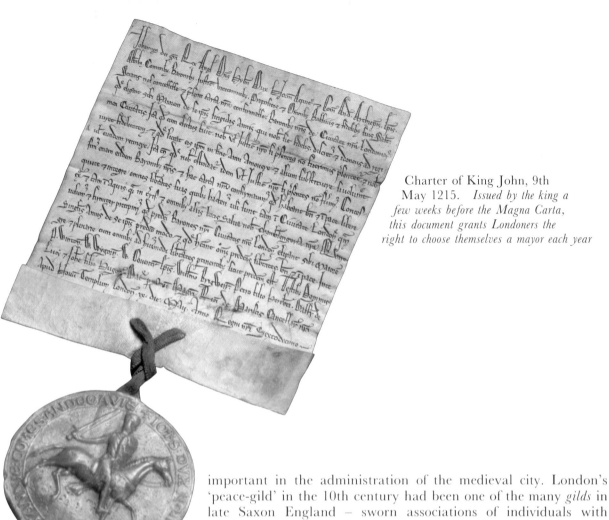

Charter of King John, 9th
May 1215. *Issued by the king a
few weeks before the Magna Carta,
this document grants Londoners the
right to choose themselves a mayor each year*

important in the administration of the medieval city. London's 'peace-gild' in the 10th century had been one of the many *gilds* in late Saxon England – sworn associations of individuals with common interests. In return for a regular subscription (the word *gild* simply means 'payment') they provided their members with support in time of trouble, collective religious ceremonies and, perhaps most attractive, regular feasts.

In towns, amid a large floating population, such gilds supplied a sense of security; they were established bodies to which a man could turn for the sort of help which in more stable rural communities he could expect from family, neighbours or feudal landlord. For many townsmen their common interests were with others in the same trade; already by 1130 there was a gild of weavers in London. Other gilds had social or charitable functions. In 1179–80 a number were listed which had been set up without the king's approval; they included several 'of the bridge', which presumably devoted their funds to work on the new stone bridge. But some had trade or craft titles; goldsmiths, pepperers, butchers. These, like the weavers' gild, although they were not the direct ancestors of any of the gilds or livery companies which in later medieval times controlled London's trade and industry, foreshadowed their development.

Thus Anglo-Saxon aldermen and gilds, Scandinavian husting and Norman-French commune and mayor came together in the 12th century to form the basic structure of London's future government.

One of London's portreeves in the early 12th century was Gilbert Becket, a merchant from Rouen who, like others from that Norman town, had established himself as a leading citizen of London. His son Thomas, born and brought up in London, became Chancellor of England and Archbishop of Canterbury, and, until their fatal argument over the relationship of church and state, a close friend and confidant of King Henry II. On 29 December 1170 Archbishop Thomas was murdered in Canterbury Cathedral by a group of knights acting, they believed, on the wishes of the king. Three years later he was canonized as a saint and martyr. In official documents he had called himself 'Thomas of London', and London quickly adopted the new saint as a patron. In the early 13th century his image, clad in his archbishop's robes, appeared on one side of the city's seal, with this short Latin verse, a prayer:

Common Seal. On the opposite face to the figure of St Paul (see page 39) was that of St Thomas Becket, enthroned over the London skyline

ME QUE TE PEPERI
NE CESSES THOMA TUERI

'May you not cease, Thomas, to protect me, (the city) that bore you'. The chapel on the new stone bridge was dedicated to St

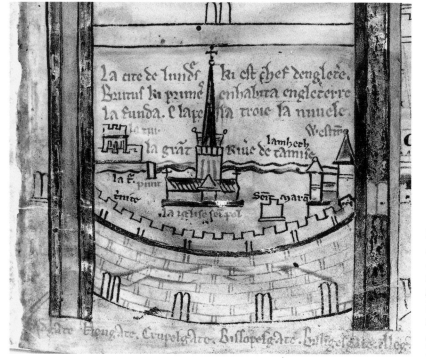

London in the 13th century. *Matthew Paris's vignette, drawn in 1252, emphasizes the notable features of the city: its wall and gates, the Tower, St Paul's, the river and bridge, and Westminster. It reminds the reader of the legend, 'Brutus, who first settled England, founded it and called it New Troy'*

Thomas; a small monastic house was founded later on the site of his birthplace in Cheapside, and a hospital in Southwark which he may himself have been instrumental in founding was renamed St Thomas' Hospital in his honour.

Among the eyewitnesses to Thomas' murder was his secretary, William Fitz Stephen ('William son of Stephen'), a fellow Londoner who had worked with him for many years. A few years later William wrote an account of the saint's life; its preface, some 2000 words of ornate Latin, consists of a description of London itself, the saint's birthplace, some of which is quoted earlier in this book. William's delight in obscure words, flowery phrases and apt (or sometimes inept) quotations from Roman authors was matched only by his enthusiasm for his home town, 'the most noble city'. To William it was the best of all possible towns, spoilt only by 'the immoderate drinking of fools and the frequency of fires'. Archaeology and documentary sources cannot readily confirm his first complaint. However, the incorporation in the realm of Henry II of England of the wine-growing region of Gascony provided a ready source of wine for the English market, and the Bordeaux wine trade was to be a major feature of London's commerce, and a major source of wealth for its merchants. The 'frequency of fires', on the other hand, is documented in chronicle accounts of the many great fires of the 11th and 12th centuries, and by legislation in the early 13th century to encourage the building of more fire-resistant houses.

The picture William presents is an idealized one, but it remains the earliest description of London by someone who knew it well. William's attitude is well represented in his first paragraph. 'Among the noble cities of the world which Fame celebrates, the city of London, seat of the monarchy of England, is the one which spreads its fame more widely, distributes its goods and merchandise further and holds its head higher'. He proceeds to describe the advantages of London's situation and its climate and the innate virtue of its citizens. Its Christian faith is evident, he thinks, in the number of churches – the 13 great monastic houses and the 126 parish churches.

London's fortifications were impressive. There was a 'palatine fortress' (the Tower) in the east, two other castles in the west. On the north side was the city wall with towers and seven 'twofold' gateways. The wall and its towers remained much as they were when built by the Romans. Defensive works of some sort had been carried out in the days of King Alfred, but only minor improvements seem to have been undertaken on the wall and its defensive ditch before the 13th century. The 'twofold' gates – perhaps William means they had two arches – may have been for the most part patched-up Roman structures; the names of two, Ludgate and Cripplegate, seem to mean narrow and crooked gates, perhaps indicating their dilapidated state at the time they received those names. One gate, however, that at Aldgate, was rebuilt early in the 12th century, while another must at least have been extensively altered to justify the name 'Newgate' it had already acquired by the 1180s. Excavation has confirmed William's statement that along the riverside the defensive wall built by the Romans had collapsed, eroded by the 'fishy River Thames'.

Pilgrim's ampulla. *This container for holy water was brought back to London by a 13th-century visitor to the shrine of St Thomas at Canterbury. On it is a scene of Thomas' murder (above) and burial (below)*

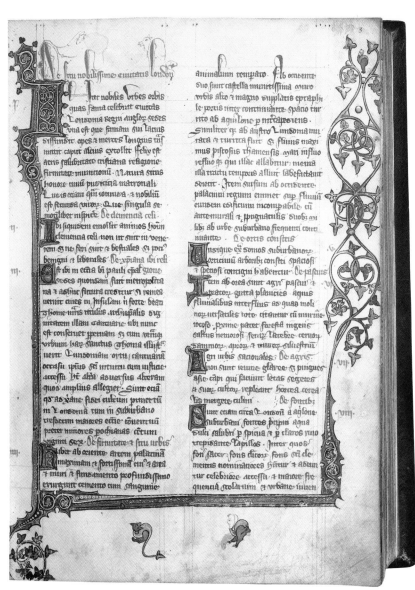

William Fitz Stephen's description of London. *The opening of a copy of the 12th-century description included in a 14th-century book of City laws and customs*

Clerkenwell. *A detail from a 16th-century map shows the site of the nunnery at Clerkenwell with the 'clerks well' to the west, one of the 'pleasant springs' to which, according to William Fitz Stephen, Londoners strolled out on summer evenings*

Beyond the walls lay an area of fields, pastures and woodland with streams and clear springs, where Londoners strolled on summer evenings. To the west at Westminster stood the royal palace, 'an incomparable building', linked to the city by a crowded suburb. Though William describes London as 'the seat of the monarchy' the idea of a political capital was to come much later. Yet the Exchequer, the department set up in the 12th century to handle the kingdom's finances, was soon based at Westminster – even though the royal treasury was at Winchester. William's statement may have been a slight exaggeration in his own day, but it foreshadowed reality.

His enthusiastic description of the schools attached to the city's chief churches – the pupils' Latin exercises as well as the cockfights they held, apparently in the schoolroom, on Shrove Tuesday – must reflect his own boyhood; 'for we were all boys once', he comments. He is equally enthusiastic about a cookshop by the river, in the area where the wine trade was carried on (the Vintry).

The riverside wall. *Excavation shows how, just as William Fitz Stephen described, the Roman wall had been eroded by the Thames. Broken stonework lies on top of the dark river silts which undermine the wall*

12th-century horseshoes. *Horses sold at the weekly markets at Smithfield were essential in war and for transport and haulage*

Here you could buy ready-cooked meals to satisfy even the most choosy of unexpected guests.

Tradesmen and craftsmen, he tells us, had their own quarters where they worked and sold their wares. This localization of particular shops and industries is a feature, though a changing one, of London's topography throughout the middle ages, and is reflected in many of the city's streetnames, such as Bread Street, Milk Street and Ironmonger Lane. One market he describes in some detail: the weekly horse and cattle fair held on the 'smooth field' (Smithfield – ancestor of the present meat market), with its impromptu horseraces to show off the animals' speed. Farmers from the countryside around London could buy livestock here as well as ploughs and any other equipment they might need.

William turns to verse to describe London's international trade:

> The Arab sends gold, the Sabaean spice and incense,
> The Scythian weapons; the fertile land of Babylon
> Sends palm-oil from its rich forests, the Nile its precious stones;
> The Chinese send purple-dyed cloths, the French their wines,
> The Norwegians and Russians send squirrel fur, miniver and
> sables.

His list sounds fanciful, but documents and archaeology agree that highly valuable imports from such exotic places were indeed reaching London in the 12th century.

London, says William, is considerably older than Rome. This apparently fanciful claim reflects the belief of medieval historians that Britain had first been colonized by a group of exiled Trojans, and that on the site of London they had founded a city called New Troy. New Troy or *Trinovantum* was the invention of the writer Geoffrey of Monmouth, whose *History of the Kings of Britain*, written in the 1130s, combined an unscrupulous misuse of historical facts with imaginative embroidery upon them; it was eagerly taken up by such writers as William Fitz Stephen, for it provided London with a glorious pedigree to match its contemporary status. For William it provided the basis for a favourable comparison of London with ancient Rome, for the legendary founders of that city also were of Trojan stock, and the same laws, he claimed, applied in each city.

From the city's origins and institutions William turns to its pleasures and pastimes: 'it is not good for a city only to be busy and serious unless it is also pleasant and merry'. He describes Shrove Tuesday football, jousting in Lent, regattas on the Thames at Easter, athletics and dancing in the summer, the baiting of boars, bulls and bears in winter. He devotes special attention to winter sports, when the marsh (the Moor or Moorfields) outside the walls to the north froze over. Young men 'more skillful at playing on the ice' would tie the shin-bones of animals to their feet as skates and push themselves along with iron-spiked sticks 'as fast as a flying bird or a javelin from a catapult'. Hunting with hawk and hound in the woods around London was popular: 'the citizens have the right to hunt in Middlesex, Hertfordshire, the whole of the Chilterns, and Kent as far as the River Cray ' – an unusual privilege in an England whose kings were jealously protective of their own hunting rights, but one which the citizens certainly claimed in the 1130s as an age-old custom, and which perhaps was given royal confirmation.

William concludes by stating that the city has produced many famous men, one of them being 'the Blessed Thomas, the archbishop Christ's glorious martyr'. Thomas' biographer was not perhaps a great writer, but the range of quotations from classical authors he includes shows him to be well-read, a credit to the London school where he was educated. He provides us with a lively picture of the city to set beside the workaday evidence of archaeology and documents. If he overlooked London's imperfections in his enthusiasm he was not the last Londoner to do so. Some 700 years after the defeated Britons fled to Roman *Londinium* out of Kent, 500 years after the earliest references to the trading activities of Saxon *Lundenwic*, and 300 years after the viking Great Army made its winter quarters there, London in the second half of the 12th century was a city which its people must have felt could justly be described, in William Fitz Stephen's words, as 'fortunate in the healthfulness of its climate, in its Christian faith, in the strength of its defences, in the nature of its situation, the honour of its citizens, and the chastity of its women'. Already a proud city, London was to experience unprecedented growth and development, though not without setbacks, in the centuries that followed.

Bone skates. *The undersides are polished by use on the ice. Found in the Moorfields area, they are of the type described by William Fitz Stephen*

Pottery jug. *This glazed and decorated jug was made in or near London in the time of William Fitz Stephen*

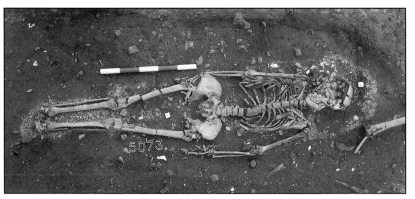

A Norman Londoner. *A grave lined with chalk and mortar in the early medieval cemetery of the church of St Nicholas Shambles, Newgate Street. This young woman died in her late twenties, when she was already suffering from osteoarthritis*